Seeking a Dwelling Beloved

Francisco Sanchez, Jr.

Published by Revival Waves of Glory Books & Publishing

PO Box 596| Litchfield, Illinois 62056 USA

www.revivalwavesofgloryministries.com

Revival Waves of Glory Books & Publishing is committed to excellence in the publishing industry.

Published in the United States of America

ISBN: 978-1-365-88441-2

Table of Contents

Acknowledgement

$\mathcal{I}$ would like very much to give great thanks to he who called me son and knowledge of son he gave me when I presented myself as son by me being born alive and by me being born alive, thus he also was reborn alive and he was reborn alive as my loving Father beloved! Thank you greatly, Father! You, loving Father, are my Master beloved!

Dedication

*S*eeking *A Dwelling Beloved* is dedicated to all of those who feel or has felt painfully lonely, for they are true vessels or empty souls to be dwellings of the great spirit of the good and loving creator. That is, if they really want to become dwellings in truth. And if in truth, they desire the great spirit of the good and the loving creator in them, thus they must seek the good and loving creator and present themselves as dwellings to the good and loving creator so that the good and loving creator puts in them with complete gladness and with complete joy the great spirit of the good and loving creator and they thus will become as new as if they had never ever really suffered painful loneliness.

Introduction

ℰvery conscious being through instincts seeks a dwelling but because of simple instincts the conscious being knows not what is that dwelling. But the truth is that the dwelling which the conscious being seeks is the very truth which will make the conscious being the truth for finding the truth. In other words, to simply enter or to simply understand which is to really find himself in the truth!

Now then, what the conscious being does by instincts is to seek in truth his very identity but the conscious being knows it not because what he does through instincts is in truth a fact without knowing or understanding. That is to say that truth knowledge knows not that true knowledge knows or that it in truth exists but true knowledge is not alive or true knowledge alone does not understand. And that is what in truth is the conscious or the living being, true knowledge!

But so that the conscious being knows or understands what he knows or what he understands thus the conscious being must do the movement to know or to understand that he knows or that he is true knowledge. And by doing the movement to know or to understand, thus the conscious being has come to enter in truth in himself!

That is to say in truth, when the conscious being comes to really understand or comes to really know, thus it will be as if the conscious being has just really arrived or has been born in that very instant but with complete or true knowledge or with complete understanding! And that true knowledge or that complete understanding is a complete dwelling, a real and complete dwelling which forever will become new or renews! And in that dwelling which forever will become new thus will come God to dwell and it will be as a second salvation because forever will dwell the spirit or the gladness of God in that conscious being who became dwelling, but dwelling in truth or real dwelling for doing the movement of knowing and of being born or of being reborn in truth or through knowledge!

Thus, one will be the glad and joyful dwelling of God, the good and loving creator. But in reality, only those to who were granted real knowledge or true knowledge or the knowledge of son beloved of God, thus can they be real dwellings of God for receiving the knowledge of real dwellings of God. That is, only those who were named or who were renamed son, beloved of God by God can be also named dwellings of God if dwelling of God they in truth desire it.

This new or true knowledge of real or of true dwelling of God is in truth as a new birth or a rebirth which also can be called resurrection because now one has been reborn again or one has being resurrected in life with the spirit of God in one. And God will dwell with all gladness and with all joy in one son beloved of God! And when God dwells in one son beloved of God thus God and one will be one!

Now then, when one becomes a real dwelling or true dwelling of God, thus one will have the knowledge or the wisdom and the understanding of God, the good and loving creator! Because the truth is that when one understands as dwelling of God, thus one is in truth in the true real tent or in the place of God the creator and for that God will be also in one!

But those who do not believe in truth or who do not have true faith of God the creator, thus what is written above about the real dwelling of God, the good and loving creator, can really be compared in truth with the next conscious mode of thinking, where if one were able to enter, thus one would be in truth as God the creator! But the truth is that if one does not believe or if one does not have faith of God, as creator, even though one believes that there is another conscious mode of thinking and that it is accessible, one will never be as God or God-man and even less can enter that next conscious mode of thinking!

Also, what is written above about the true dwelling of God can really be compared with the atom or in the way in which the atom works. Normally in the atom, the electrons go around the nucleus or the negative goes around the positive or the protons as the moon or even a cloud goes around the earth. In other words, the small goes around the great. But in the case of the real or true dwelling of God, the protons or the positive or the nucleus goes around the electrons or goes around the small or act together! That is to say, all the parts of the atom work as a single piece and for that reason, the atom will not stop working or stop from changing from one type of atom or element into another atom or another element because it will always be atom or matter or the element number one. That is to say, the atom or the element will not disintegrate or will not stop from existing because the atom or every element in the universe will really stop from existing!

So, therefore, seek to be a dwelling in truth or to be a true dwelling of God, the good and loving creator, because as a true dwelling of God thus everything will become as new, even God Himself will become as new!

One is Knowledge

One is knowledge and when one is born, one also brings forth knowledge of life or one brings forth knowledge of dead. If one is born dead, thus one brings knowledge of dead to the world and because of one bringing knowledge of dead to the world thus knowledge of dead is given to one and later one is forgotten, as if one were never born and if one is remembered afterward, thus it was for the real pain which remained with the living.

And if one is born alive then one brings forth true gladness and true joy which revives in truth those who waited for one but one also for being born alive brings forth true knowledge of life to the world and through that very same knowledge which one brought forth or which one presented to the world. Thus, one also in truth will be known and one through the very same knowledge of one thus one will also be able in truth to receive more true or more real knowledge. And according to what in truth one does with that new knowledge, thus one will truly be reborn!

Now then, to be reborn simply is to receive or simply is to be granted real knowledge from above with all power and with all authority over life which now is salvation!

So, therefore, if one does not present oneself in life with real or with true knowledge, thus one will not receive in life real knowledge or true knowledge so that oneself can be reborn in life and in life have the true power of salvation and continue in life and also be able to keep and maintain.

One is Life

One is life for one, even though one can give life to another but that life to another is not for one but for that other. One is for one as another is for that other! No one is ever for another as another is never for one.

Life is an empty vase which many others call soul; they call it soul because they really know not the real meaning behind the soul. And still some others call life spirit or something that cannot be seen because life is only known through the motion that life does itself for itself.

Now then, life or the soul or the spirit is an empty vase or an empty vessel that has to be filled and transformed in life before life or the soul or the spirit dies and loses the ability to be life or the soul or the spirit. For life is a simple and empty vessel that has to be filled!

And an empty vessel has very few stains and is very easy to clean and to fill. But a vessel stained with false knowledge is a vessel very difficult to fill but a vessel very easy to lose. And once one as life, which is an empty vessel, is lost thus one is lost for all eternity!

Thus, praise the maker of life because salvation is because of the praise that one makes to the maker of life. And the maker of life is the only one who can fill one for all times because of the praised one.

To Send and To Be

Because one was sent does not mean that one came from another place, even though it may be true that one was really sent! And that which once was really separated to bring true gladness and true joy after the great affliction, that will never ever be united again because of the true gladness and the true joy that will come after the great affliction due to the separation, thus that will become as new and as if it never ever was really separated and really afflicted!

So, therefore, in truth no one will ever go anywhere after death! But when he is reborn with true knowledge in life, thus he will feel as if he has just really arrived from another place because everything has become as if new!

The Earth and the Fall

If in truth there were no earth, thus in truth nothing would ever fall because there would not even be a single sky. For, in truth, there is only sky because of the earth and the sky by itself there is not and everything which falls thus falls to the earth because the earth is the one which receives the affliction because of the separation. And when the earth is reborn by new and true knowledge, thus the earth will become as if a new earth and the sky thus also will become as a second sky and the sky will become as two skies. And every time that the earth is reborn, thus also the skies!

Now then, until now there are three skies because the earth has been reborn two times!

As Double Reward

He who really wants good things in truth, he must labor joyfully and when they arrive or when they become complete not only will he receive them joyfully but he also will receive them as double reward.

When the Voice is Not Seen

One cannot respond to what one knows not no matter how sweet in truth the voice may sound! Our instinct makes us look for who is calling us so that we first can know who is really calling and according to our now new knowledge thus respond. But when the voice is not seen, thus to the voice is not responded.

But a voice which calls one through one's very own name, even though that voice cannot be seen, is a voice calling one to give true knowledge to one so that with true knowledge thus one can see the true voice!

Now then, when one in truth becomes beloved of God, thus one will be called by God away from one but God will not say that it is God calling! And if one does not respond, the voice will become silent. And so that the voice of God calls one again, thus one must do as son beloved so that one as son beloved is called and as son beloved one responds. But if one does not respond, no matter how many times the voice calls, then one will lose salvation when one really dies for not responding!

Because in truth, God will call his servant beloved as son beloved that way taking him from affliction and giving him salvation so that as son beloved of God, he can live with all abundance of life alive and all power over her!

Learning and Attention

One learns in truth a lot more with only in truth one lending attention with all gladness and with all joy. But if one does not feel glad and joyful before learning, thus one can still in truth feel glad and joyful because one will learn or really know something new!

Now then, the greater part of attention is really one and when one becomes glad and joyful because one is going to receive new knowledge that new knowledge can be true knowledge or can be royal knowledge. And with true or royal knowledge, thus life is saved alive!

When Everything is Possible

Everything is possible for those who have but if they cannot see the lack through what they have, thus everything in truth will be lost, even they themselves!

To see the lack or the fault, thus one must look toward above where in truth everything is minus one. And one must also add to everything with one. But one will never ever in truth go up to where everything minus one is because things come down to the earth and the heavens forever will be without one. And the truth is that when one adds to what already is complete thus what already is complete will come to one so that one is as in the heavens and also as complete.

Now then, one adds to what already is complete by asking for grace! Because in truth, to ask for or to give grace is in truth asking for the loving grace of he who made the heavens complete minus one and put one on the earth so that one could ask for his loving grace and through his loving grace, one is reborn or one becomes new so that also everything, as the heavens and one also, become forever and ever new with all the loving presences which makes everything possible.

Learning and Believing

To learn is also to believe and to believe is seeing that there is really more here on earth where one is and one is alive. The heavens are only for the things of the heavens and the earth is for the things of the earth and even though the heavens became complete through the very separation of the earth from the heavens, the heavens lack the earth which makes possible the heavens as the earth lacks the heavens.

But so that the earth can be complete as the very heavens, the earth must request the heavens for true knowledge of the heavens and when the heavens grants true knowledge to the earth, thus not only will the earth be as in the heavens but also the heavens will be as other heavens.

Now then, the earth in truth is one and one is the dust which he who made heaven and completed heaven through the very separation of the earth so that heaven became as a new heaven, the dust that he desires with all gladness and with all joy, before it becomes dark again and life stops from being, to rise up and say, Fathers!

Because in truth, that is the power of God that the dust rises in life and in life says as son with all true gladness and with all true joy and with all true gladness and with all true joy God will say as Fathers!

I Have Much to Learn

I have much to learn from you, my loving Master and my God! I have much to learn from you, my loving Master and my God! But my loving Master how am I to learn if you, my loving Master and my God, do not teach me as a loving Father? And, loving Master, if you teach me not, how am I going to do as son to understand the things of God as Father?

Because my loving Master and my God, if I understand not or I do not receive true or royal knowledge from you, then you, my loving Master, will never declare me your son beloved so that in truth I, as your son beloved, can really triumph and can really rest in your true joy of Father as it is your very great pleasure!

Of Nothing Serves a Poor Wise Man

It is much easier for a town to listen to a rich man even though he may be very stupid or even though he may be very foolish than it is for a town to listen in truth to a wise but poor man no matter how much the town needs the wisdom.

Thus, the truth makes no one rich until that no one becomes the very truth because of the truth and the very truth will speak riches for that no one.

Now then, wisdom is in truth smalls warnings that here on the very earth is much more in truth of what one really can see. And wisdom is so that the wise prepares to see in truth what cannot be seen without wisdom.

Seeking a Dwelling Beloved

Prayer for Prosperity

My loving Master and my God, for the great and true love that you have toward your beloved, please grant me a blessing in my hands so that I, through your loving grace, my loving Master and my God, will be able to prosper although through the very sweat of my body and forever I will be grateful to you!

For the Joy of Another

Many times for the joy or for the pleasure which another brings to one, thus one takes abuse from that other, loves one that other or not!

But true joy or true pleasure as also is the love which is true, thus forever is renewed, he who loves as also he who is loved or beloved.

Without Royal Knowledge

If one has not true or royal knowledge of God, the good and loving creator, thus in truth there is no total or true or royal happiness! Because in truth, in the very same manner which true or royal love in truth renews thus also in truth total or true or royal happiness!

Recognizing a Greater Greatness

It is impossible to be great without recognizing a greater greatness. Because in truth, he who really became great, recognized a greater greatness and the greater greatness recognized him also as great so that he in truth could be great!

The Spirit and the Soul

The good and loving spirit or the royal gladness of God is in truth sweet and dwells not in a bitter vessel or soul. The good and loving spirit or the royal gladness of God is also alive and neither dwells in a dead vessel or dead soul.

So, therefore, seek in truth God who is alive so that God revives your soul alive with all joy of God alive!

To Teach and to Learn

No teacher, no matter how wise, can teach if the student will not enjoy in truth to learn or to know. Because in truth, the joy or the desire is the key which in truth takes and which in truth brings without having to do the motion of going and of arriving.

Owner and Master

He who is the owner of illusions, fantasies or hypocrisy, is no master.

God is my Master!

God is my Master beloved and my Master beloved has left me with a load which I have to know in truth! But I have to wait for my Master God beloved to return and unload me! And God will unload me with true knowledge of son beloved because in truth God is my Master beloved!

With the Pleasures of the Skin

Many say that God is their Lord but none serve God! They only serve the vain doctrine of their hearts with the pleasures of the skin which in truth is the lord of vanity!

Chapter 2

To Do and to Respond

According to the true knowledge of life or the name which one received for bringing to the world true knowledge of one and also bringing true knowledge of life, thus to one also was given true knowledge. And with that new and true knowledge thus one will do in truth and one will respond in truth in the world!

Now then, if one comes not to do and responds not when one is called from above with the true knowledge or name given or granted to one, thus in truth one will die! But before one dies, obviously, one will be called again to see if one comes one day to respond, but if one responds not, thus no longer will one be able to respond because one will die and death will respond for one for one being dead! That is, the dead will respond for dead and will never respond for living and the living who does not respond in life, life he will stop from having! Therefore, do through the knowledge given or granted so that you can be called in life and in life you respond! Because in truth, if one does not respond in life thus there will not be salvation and if there is no salvation thus neither will there be dwelling of God in one forever!

The True Sacrifice

The true sacrifice which God desires from one is that one becomes joyful in truth with the joy of God. That is the true sacrifice! That is the true surrender because in truth both parts will enjoy the joy of God as one.

Now then, with the joy of God in one, thus not only one can revive in life but also one can revive God and for reviving God, God will save one in life with double abundance of life, double abundance of life because God will be in one!

Heaven Will Be Filled With Hypocrites

According to the doctrine of man, heaven will be filled with hypocrites! And if heaven will be filled with hypocrites, then I there want not to go, even if in truth one can get there!

Because in truth, according also to the doctrine of man, many go to heaven but the doctrine of man says not how many arrive!

Knowledge and Hypocrisy

He who in truth knows hypocrisy and in truth he does not get away from her, thus he also is a hypocrite and because of his hypocrisy he will pay dearly!

Now then, hypocrisy is to live contrary to what comes out from the mouth or is to do very contrary to the faith. It is to say that one loves the world when in truth one loves no body, not even a single one!

And when the hypocrisy is discovered, he who discovered he never ever will be the same because he is now as if the very truth! And he who is a hypocrite is now as if an opened grave, which smells so bad!

As Son and as Fathers

The great majority envy the way a good and loving father loves and takes good care of a son, but none of the great majority of them do as son and even less do as father. Hypocrites! Yes, hypocrites! Hypocrites, because in truth we all have the great power to love and the great power also of taking good care as sons and as fathers!

New Thanks

Thank you, my loving God and my Master, for blessing my two hands to prosper! For in truth, my Master God, I am working with them and with them as also with my very own voice with all gladness and with all joy I will raise them and I will give new thanks to you!

Lost Son

When a son, even though son beloved, shows no respect for others, not even to the elders, thus it is because the father has shown lack of respect in not instructing the son through the good road, thus that son, even though beloved, not instructed is a lost son.

A Man with Royal Joy

When a man with joy of God is reborn son beloved of God through the knowledge of son beloved of God, thus no only also is God reborn but also the times are reborn because the times were reborn for the son beloved.

A Borrowed Thought

A borrowed thought or a borrowed idea cannot be shared as true knowledge or as truth because one is the greater part of knowledge as one is also the greater part of the truth. And since one is not part of a borrowed thought or a borrowed idea, thus one cannot be part of the truth because one was not reborn through the truth. One is reborn through the truth through the truth that one has already presented when born alive.

God and Freedom

God truly is free and God is true freedom. No man alive without God is ever free and while alive, that man alive still can be truly free but truly free through God. And all dead men have lost the chance to be free because they serve death by being dead!

One and Amplification

Without one in truth there is no amplification. For in truth, the more one is in reality, in realty the more is the amplification. Now then, to amplify is in truth to add to creation with the knowledge presented to one through the knowledge of life which one presented by being born alive, because more knowledge is given to one for being born alive!

There is Joy of God!

A virgin is the true joy of God which always remains new and when she is known in truth, thus she renews in truth and everything becomes as new, as if it never were before without joy.

There is true joy of God and virgin she is in truth and she will give rebirth to one and one will be reborn as if the only son ever and everything will become as if new, new as if one never were born but forever were in the true joy of God.

As if it Were Nothing

If nothing is complete, well then, it is as if it were nothing. To understand or to know the good word and do nothing and not achieve with her is as if one understood not or as if one knew not. Because in truth, to come to know the good word is in truth to come to live the true life!

Now then, in truth one sees according to what one is and the more or the better knowledge one has, thus better in truth one will be and one in truth will see!

The Mind and the Body

When the mind is heavy with burden, the body returns not complete. And sometimes when the complete body returns, the mind has yet to arrive. One feels as if something was really left behind and one must run out and get it in the good rest.

Death and True Freedom

As long as there is death, there is no true freedom. To die really was to lose the battle for life and to lose also all possibility to true freedom, true freedom which is God alive.

Now then, God is one and because of one God is God! And one alive is in truth the one who makes all possibility…

Surviving and Life

Surviving in truth is not to live, for in truth is a very poor imitation of life which cannot be seen! And also one cannot in truth imitate what one knows not and much less one can in truth imitate if it cannot be seen.

Now then, true knowledge really allows one to see so that one can in truth imitate and with that very imitation one can in truth understand or one can in truth make the true belief even more complete. Because in truth, through true belief or through true knowledge one lives in truth and as the very truth!

To Seek and to Find

He who seeks in truth finds in truth but only and when he knows what he is seeking! If one seeks and one finds not then it is because it is not in one! And if one has but what one has does not make one happy, then it was never for one!

Thus, throw a side everything which does not make you happy that is of no need. Never throw a side your sons, even though they may call you stranger! And seek the truth and the truth will make you happy. And the truth is God and is in life. When you seek to believe in God, thus believe that in God you will come to believe and in God you will come to believe because God will let Himself be found from you!

As Knowing Nothing

No matter how much math one really knows if the math adds not to really much then it is as if really knowing nothing. For, to count is to name what already is and if one has counted for nothing then nothing comes to count or to name.

Creation and Division

Creation really functions the following way. Creation divides while at the very same time creation multiplies through subtraction and all the subtracted adds as true creation.

To Enter in Joy

Today is a good day, my God beloved and my loving Master! Today is a good day, my God beloved and my loving Master! And how I would enjoy joyfully entering into your true joy! But if you, my God beloved and my loving Master, do not call me son beloved and tell me to enter into your joy, I will never be able to be in truth happy as you are forever truly happy!

Today is a good day, my God beloved and loving Master! And how I would truly enjoy entering into your true joy as is your good and true pleasure!

Let the Tests Begin!

Oh, let the tests begin! Oh, let the tests begin! Because in truth, I know that you my God beloved and my loving Master will never put a test in my road which I cannot overcome according to your good pleasure!

Oh, let the tests begin! Because with every test which I joyfully pass, more righteous I will be in truth before you, my God beloved and my loving Master! Oh, let the tests begin! Oh, let the tests begin!

Chapter 3

To Draw Near and Be Chosen

According to the true answer which one responds with when one is in truth called with voice from above, thus one will be chosen and one will be united to the voice which calls in truth to grant true peace and true knowledge to one. And the union of one in truth will be felt because one will feel glad and joyful, something which one never felt before and that feeling can be called in truth the grace or the loving grace of God.

Thus that which one now really feels for being near and united to the voice or untied through the voice is called the grace, which in truth is the loving presence or the essence which cannot be really seen but it is really felt physically in one with all gladness and with all joy and also with complete or true peace. The loving grace of God in one does not bring to one the lease fear or the lease terror, but brings true gladness and true joy and even also bring true peace. But there are other people who call glory the loving grace but the glory is to physically be able to see the loving presence. But the very curious thing about the glory or the physical presence is that it cannot be seen unless one already has previous knowledge, which really is the loving grace that one feels. In other words, one will see the glory through the loving grace which one once felt through drawing near and being illuminated and through the loving grace one in truth is granted the true knowledge of servant beloved of God or son beloved of God.

Thus in truth, when a living being in truth seeks God thus that living being draws near or that living being is granted to draw near and through drawing near that living being in truth begins to feel but a very profound peace or a true peace and through that true peace he will have true knowledge of God. And that true knowledge of God will also bring him true gladness and true joy of God. And according to what he does with that gladness and with that joy, thus he will be called once again but if he does not respond, he will have to wait so that he once again can draw near and be illuminated and feel the peace and the gladness and the joy which was true or real. Now then, the gladness and the joy was so that one could be reborn in life but if one was not reborn as son beloved, even so in truth one was reborn as beloved of God!

Because in truth, through the joy of God, is in truth that he who seeks God will feel again the loving grace of God and through the loving grace he who seeks will also receive more true knowledge of God.

Now then, that rue knowledge of God can be the knowledge of son beloved of God and because of receiving the knowledge of son beloved, thus he has received also salvation! And through salvation thus he will be able to save others who are still alive. That is, in truth salvation is for the living and the living who really desire salvation and for salvation they request.

Believe and Founding

Believing is in truth like assembling a solid foundation. And when in truth one assembles a solid foundation, thus one seeks for those who know how to assemble in a foundation. And if they cannot add to your foundation, thus keep seeking!

If your foundation brings you true joy, then never knock it down! Because in truth, if your foundation is made through seeking the truth, the truth adds to the truth and the truth you will be.

A Foundation in God

He who assembles a belief or a foundation because of someone else, thus soon he will fall and very great will be his fall and no one will consul him, no one! Because in truth, that belief or that foundation was not assembled in truth or in God!

Obligated through Obligation

He who comes out from obligation through obligation, thus he will become in truth! For, he who is obligated into freedom, he is still a slave because of the lack of peace and the lack of knowledge of freedom!

Fighting for Pleasure

He who fights for his very pleasure, thus he at the end will lose! For, he will be fighting himself! For, true pleasure comes and renews automatically when one has being victorious for the things of God.

When Understanding Rests

To have understanding or true knowledge, thus the things are known and the things are seen completely formed because knowledge gives form being true form itself. And when the understanding or the knowledge rests, thus the things known hide, that way creating chaos!

But when the understanding or the knowledge is reborn, thus the things are also reborn and they no longer hide because now they have complete form!

The Computer and the Human

Of no value is the computer if there is no human to compute. Moreover, the human is a true computer and when he finds out his true purpose, the truth will speak in truth for the human and of nothing will serve the computer or the tablet or even the capsule!

To Renew the Creator

Of nothing really serves creation if there is not a living man to not only renew creation, but also to renew the creator. Because in truth, man has really the power in life as son beloved to renew the creator to Father beloved!

Because in truth, God the creator is revived as beloved in everyone who is alive!

The Intersection and Man

The intersection was before man and not man before the intersection. In fact, man is the only true intersection! The only thing which connects God to creation is man! And without man in creation, thus there is no intersection to unite God to creation of God or unite creation to God.

For Man was Creation

For man was creation and creation was man but man was really dust and through the power of creation, dust would get up as a living being and as a living being praise creation and the power of creation and dust as a living being would praise that power as God.

And that power of God was that, that dust would get up and praise God for creating! But that does not stay there! For God will reward man again with life if man again praises God and praises God as loving Father for man was creation of God!

Over Extending

If you over extend your arm, your arm you will break! If you over extend the word, the word you will twist thus making the word useless, unresponsive and uncreative and very painful! So, therefore, keep your mouth shut if you are not praising to bring higher!

Over-filled Vase

He who surpasses in understanding is as he who knows nothing, for an over-filled vase throws away the very best...

Now then, to understanding was to have entered into the grandiose tent of the loving Father and in there feel refreshed with complete gladness and with complete joy and feel also as if one were never ever outside the tent…

The Very Best Vase

It is very wise to have two vases, one to fill and the other to empty. But the very best vase is that vase which fills as it empties. And that vase is one, because one becomes truly complete as one divides to multiply and when there is one left, it is because one has subtracted a lot to be truly complete!

To Choose is to Complete

Meditation or belief means getting before the intersection before death and thus making the right turn, if there is any right turn to make. To go through is to come after but to choose is to truly complete or to become as first despite of the many others that already did.

False Belief

One can tell that the belief of another is a false belief when he prefers to be somewhere else, even away from his belief for his belief is in life while alive!

Thus, a true heaven believer is one who wants true heaven on earth as in the beginning!

Division and Separation

Dividing or separation competes nothing but understanding or knowing does; knowing that because of the division or the separation one in truth has become as new when before united one knew not or one understood not that there was one and that one was one. He who has stayed away from hypocrisy.

He, even though late in his life, that in truth has stayed away from hypocrisy, he has done more than enough in his life! He has done more in truth than those who believe themselves to be holy.

Because in truth, only God Himself can declare holiness for only God is holy and only God can justified or name one as holy…

Before Dying

Although once in life, obviously before dying, seek he who looks at everything and everything he sees so that you can see that there is more on earth than you can imagine!

That is, to look at everything is not to see everything! But to know is to see everything even see he who looks and sees!

Those Who Deny the Truth

The truth brings controversy to all of those who deny the truth, who do not want the truth and who neither seek the truth. But the truth adds to those who honestly seek the truth for being the truth.

Where is the Knowledge?

My God beloved and my loving Master, where is the knowledge of son beloved which I ask of you so that I can know as son and you declare me also son beloved and that way also I can overcome and triumph in your true joy of Father as is your good pleasure?

My God beloved and my loving Master, where is the knowledge of son beloved of God which I ask of you? My loving Master, for your great love toward your beloved, please grant me and both of us will be free from the desolation!

There is No Greater Joy!

There is no greater joy than yours, my God beloved and my loving Master! There is no greater joy than yours, my God beloved and my loving Master, because your true joy stays, thus making one as new and also pushes one in truth toward you, my God beloved and my loving Master! There is no greater joy than the joy of God as Father beloved!

Chapter 4

Salvation is through Praise

No son who is not known says to an unknown, father! The son who is born alive not only brings true knowledge of son, but also he brings true knowledge of life alive and because of bringing true knowledge of son alive thus to him also is given true knowledge or name of living son so that with true knowledge of son alive he odes for life and when he is called, he responds father because he knows who is really calling through doing or for being born son!

Now then, he who in truth will be saved will be saved through the true praise which comes out from his mouth because true salvation is through the praise which comes out through his very own mouth!

Because in truth, according to the true knowledge which one brought into the world at birth thus through that very same knowledge one has to do to be reborn and because of being reborn, receive also true knowledge or acknowledgement of son, but of son beloved of God.

Once more, true salvation is through true praise which comes out from one's very own mouth before one dies and one remains forever silent!

When There is Nothing to Read

When there is nothing else to read, then it is time to take out the pen and write, write and write!

Now then, read all that can be really read and that which cannot be really remembered reading thus write that!

God is Joy

To know God is gladness and joy and is truth. And a glad and a joyful contender pleases God in truth.

Grant me your loving grace!

My God beloved and my loving Master, how I would enjoy that you as loving Father grant me your loving grace! My God beloved and my loving Master, please increase your joy in me because your joy will being me your loving grace and your loving grace will bring me your rename!

Wisdom as Subscription

Those who subscribe to God receive wisdom of heart as their subscription.

If We Could Hear Our Voices!

How joyful would my day be, my God beloved and my loving Master, if only we in truth could hear our voices! I praise you and according to my praise toward you, you God will respond to me that way making my day more joyful!

How joyful would my day be, my God beloved and my loving Master, if in truth we could hear our voices!

Grant me knowledge!

How much lovelier, how much lovelier would be my day if you my God would allow me to hear your voice, that way making me a bit more joyful and thus relieving also a bit more this struggle to know and to overcome and that way also to rest and to triumph in your true joy as loving Father as it is your good pleasure!

Interest and Books

He who is not interested in books, thus of nothing in truth serves him to go or to enter a library because through him the library will not be complete. Because in truth, a library is more complete through the interest of one in books than all the books which are in the library!

That which is of God is Life

When a false prophet, of those who choose themselves to lie for profit, speaks thus the majority of the people lend ear but they worry, thus fearing to die! But the interesting thing is that those who lend ear do not do that which is of God, which is in truth to live!

Not until One Seeks

One cannot in truth live not until one seeks in truth he who grants life and he who grants life is found in truth and he grants life which is in truth the salvation of he!

To Die and to Live

Many fear to really die, but they are not willing to really do to really live and for not really doing thus they really die! Now then, to really do will put one in need to really know but to really know or to come to know will really allow one to live because to come to know in truth will do all the living one needs to do in truth!

Thus in truth what irony that the great majority fear in truth to die but in truth they do not do to know in truth and in truth live!

Wisdom Brings More Wisdom

Even though knowledge can leave one dumbfounded, wisdom of heart in truth brings more wisdom of heart and also wisdom of heart makes one joyful and joy is very essential for one to be reborn in life and be reborn as savior of life.

Being Wise

Knowing or being smart does not really mean being wise. It is just that, knowing or being smart; for wisdom of heart really comes or is really granted from far and really comes from above. And as soon as one begins to look for wisdom of heart, one will find it in the heart, put there by the good and loving Creator of true knowledge from above.

What is That is Known?

What is that is known in truth but one must do in truth to in truth know and in truth thus victory can be declared to one so that one can in truth overcome?

What one must know in truth is that in life there is more of what one can see in truth and that one must ask for knowledge to see that which is but cannot be seen. One does not have to really understand, but only know that one can ask and it will be granted to one but it will be granted to one through the true knowledge which one has of one…

A Day of Victories!

My God beloved and my loving Master, today would be for both of us a day of victories if your voice would tell me, come and unite to me, my son beloved!

Where is the Royal Knowledge?

Where is my God beloved and my loving Master? Where is my God beloved and my loving Master the knowledge of son beloved of God which I request to know the things of God and you God declare me victory so that I can overcome and triumph in your royal joy as loving Father, as it is your good pleasure?

My loving God and my Master beloved, where is the royal knowledge which only you as loving Father can grant me?

A Brother in Vain

A man can declare another as brother even though he may not be but if the father of that first man does not affirm it then in truth that second man is a brother in vain!

The Royal Purpose of the Creation

God is my Master beloved and how I enjoy in truth being his servant beloved, even in this desolation! Oh, how I would truly enjoy also doing His good and royal pleasure! Oh, how I would truly enjoy having the royal knowledge of God so that

I can come out from this desolation to understand or to enter in the things of God and God declare me victory for doing in truth with that royal knowledge of God and that way also I can truly overcome, triumph and rest in His true joy as it is the royal purpose of the creation of God!

My Master is my Royal Knowledge!

God is my Master beloved and my royal knowledge and also my understanding! God is my Master beloved and my true joy and my true pleasure! God is my Master beloved and God my Master beloved is my only and true salvation and my Master beloved will really save me alive in life!

Servant Beloved until Told

God is my Master beloved and I am His servant beloved and how I would truly enjoy with all my heart, with all my soul and with all my strength, which God Himself has given me to be in truth His servant beloved until God my Master says son beloved!

Chapter 5

Tests and More Tests!

What comes out from the mouth of one can really put one in tests and more tests and very contrary to what one really does. Thus in truth, when one is born, one of two things can really happen. If one is born dead, then there will be a lot of sadness for those who waited to receive one, but the sadness will be forgotten within a short time as also the dead will be forgotten once the dead is thrown to a side.

If one is born alive, then one not only has brought into the world true knowledge of life but also one has brought true gladness and true joy to all of those who waited for one. Moreover, by one simply being born alive thus also one has revived many others! Now a woman has really being reborn as mother and a man has really being reborn as father and the rest of the family also were reborn or revived.

But when one has grown up and becomes a man, then what comes out from the mouth of one can in truth revive one or can put one in tests and more tests! The tests and more tests are to simply see if in truth what comes out from one's mouth is the truth. That is to say, to see if in truth when one says father is in truth father! And if in truth one says father, then the true labors of one will respond for one. And because of the true labors of one thus one will be called in truth and the only thing in truth which one has to say is, I am here and I hear you, my Master!

And that will really be the test of tests…

True Knowledge is Knowable

True knowledge is eventually knowable or really granted. God is true knowledge and eventually God will be completely knowable in life because God is also life.

Now then, all of those who have come to die, they all have also lose the great opportunity of in truth knowing the knowable God.

Come and Unite!

My God beloved and my loving Master, how your beloved would truly enjoy being able to hear your great voice again but this time of times saying to me, come and unite to me, your God and your Master, my son beloved!

He Who is More Evil

Evil is he who lies but even more evil is he who chooses the lie and the lie takes and the lie brings.

God and One Alive

God in truth desires one alive. Because as long as one lives, thus in truth one can repent and one can do the true joy of God through the true knowledge of God! Now then, to repent in truth was to change the mind of one for the mind of son beloved!

To end, God in truth is for one alive and if one repents thus one is for God as God is for one!

The Doctrine for the Word

Those who do not renounce the doctrine for the word, they become rotten and later die without knowing the truth which always was before them and which could give them more life and even also give them the salvation of God so that they could continue with more life as savior beloved of God.

When the light arrives

When the light arrives, even the very blind know it! But the blind know it not because of the warmth of the light, but they know it because their souls, even though blind and empty, have come out from darkness to humble for more in the very light which they cannot see but that shines because of them!

The Rich and the Poor

A man with true gladness and with true joy, even though a poor man, can conquer any woman or can have a better life! But a man with true sadness, even though a rich man, loses any woman or loses any good life!

Because in truth, true gladness and true joy bring forth rebirth or renew all of those that true gladness and true joy touch!

But sadness departs even the most mature…

However, true gladness and true joy come only from God but God will grant true gladness and true joy to one for one honestly seeking God so that one as God can be reborn in abundance from gladness and from joy…

Smile!

Smile, for something better waits for you if you really wait for it for doing for it! Because in truth, waiting is the other part of doing if one has done for waiting…

The Good Fix

When something breaks, for sure someone will make money of the broken thing even if he cannot fix it but still it was a good fix…

The Greatest of Struggles

The greatest of all struggles is the surrender to God, but the surrender to God with all gladness and with all joy of God, which only God can grant and will grant to those who truly struggle to know of God.

The greatest of all warriors is he who gladly and joyfully surrenders to God because he the great warrior truly knows what is God all about.

Now then, there is no better or truer seducer than God because once God has allowed the joy of God in one, thus there is no other joy for one!

Thus, make God your true joy and your true pleasure and all the world will humble to you as you have done to God!

When the Good Will Be

Humble to the good and the good one truly will have but humble to evil and one will truly have evil. But to humble to the good is thus to humble for more and more one will have to not only live but to also relive or revive as if always new.

For What Remains

For peel or detached skin one cries not, but rather, one cries for what remains because there will be more and once more is, the peel or the detached will not be ever remembered.

Blinded in the Light

When sight is granted to a blind man, he now begins to stumble where once he did not stumble; for now he cannot recognize in the good light his very spirit. But once the once blinded comes to know or to understand the good light, thus the once blinded will no longer be blinded in the light.

Once again, when a blind man is granted sight, thus now he stumbles with sight where he did not stumble before with blindness because now he must have knowledge of light to walk in the light.

Effort and Interest

When someone pretends to look for the truth and he asks one where one found the truth, thus obviously he never sought, not even once! Because the truth is really found with effort and with interest and when the truth is really found, the truth also is understood because now one is the very truth!

Seeking a Dwelling Beloved

When One Truly Loves

True love is when one loves and everyone else looks like he who is beloved of one. And that is true love to see he who one loves in everything and in others!

The Word and the Enemy

He who tricks or who traps with words is the enemy of life. But the enemy of life tricks or traps with what one already knows or even believes…

The Best Place

The best place or dwelling is truly that place or dwelling which has become united through tests, through temptations and even through trials because truly now nothing will be able to separate that place or dwelling or take it apart to completely destroy it and leave it breathless…

Like a House without Walls

A woman who is not affectionate, even though a beautiful woman, is like a house without walls! And a house without walls is a house without warmth and because of lack of warmth, the walls fell…

Francisco Sanchez, Jr.

United through Tests

Those two who are united through tests, those two not even death can separate them; for even though death may take one, he who remains will be and will do in truth as if two!

Chapter 6

To Struggle and to Overcome

After the tests and many more tests, thus comes or arrives the good struggle to overcome and to struggle in truth. And even though one has passed with all true gladness and with all true or real joy, thus there will not be victory until victory is really declared from above!

The most interesting thing is that victory declared is now in the form of true peace or real peace which one feels as also one feels true gladness and true joy, but since one does not know in truth as to why the true gladness and the true joy, thus one now struggles to know the motive for the peace, the gladness and the true joy which now appears as chaos. Thus, it is as if smiling without knowing as to why or to be full without eating. But even so, it is still a victory even though a victory to know the truth!

That is to say, to come to struggle to know the things of God is a victory!

The Best of Memories

The best memory is that which one carries in the heart and not in the mind or in the body or one keeps in a closet, because the body is peeled and the mind is discharged and that which is kept in a closet is forgotten if not seen but the memory in the heart revives the body as also revives the mind. Thus, to remember another when one feels a simple itch in one of one's hand palms is a memory which one carries in the heart.

Knowing is forming

To really triumph or to overcome, one has to know and to know or to come to know was to give as receive complete form.

Until They Become Complete through Truth

Those who know and come to understand the word in truth, they are now as the truth, they are the very truth! But as long as they are in the word or in the truth until they become complete through the truth as the truth and once they have being completed as the very truth, thus the very truth will do and will speak for them as the light truly does and truly speaks for the son, the son beloved.

To Know as Son of the Master

Soon now, God who is my Master beloved will grant me the knowledge of son beloved as only God my Master and Father can grant so that I can know the things of God!

And when I truly know the thing of God, thus God my Master beloved will declare me son beloved so that I can already triumph and truly rest in the true joy which is God, as it is the good pleasure of God as loving Father!

Yes, soon now, God who is my Master beloved will grant me the knowledge of son beloved so that I can truly know as son beloved of the Master!

Naked Shadow

A father or even a husband who does not love is really like a tree without leaves creating a shadow which in truth benefits no one. That is to say in truth, a father who does not love is an unknown father and an unknown father is a son unknown and a son unknown do without really knowing and doing without knowing is doing and is living in vanity and living in vanity is to die and to die was for not knowing.

Easy Things

To he who things come easily or without struggling for them, he thus uses them to really deceive or to mark or to seduce those who have them not. But when the rest come to really have things through themselves, then the things of he will stop from being because they never were truly his because he never shared or divided them so that they would multiply and he now would also have more.

Without Rename

God, without your rename, I your beloved of God have lived in vain and because of living in vain thus I your beloved of God simply will die and eternally I will be dead and out from you!

True Joy

He who began the true gladness and the true joy in one, thus only He will assure to complete that true gladness and that true joy which He once begun in one; but one has to desire that true gladness and that true joy of He in one and do gladly and joyfully for them because true gladness and true joy give rebirth to one as son beloved of He and to He as Father beloved of one.

A Better Son

A son who seeks for his father, thus that son will be a better son as also the father thus will be a better father. In the very same manner, the creation which seeks its creator thus that creation will be a better creation as its creator will be a better creator.

The Struggle to Know

The lack or the need does not make one, but rather, the struggle to know the lack or the need makes one or gives form to one so that with that form one does and the lack or the need stops from being.

Now then, a lack or a need does not cover another lack or another need. Thus, he who marks or stains his body is because he wants to cover the lack or the need which is in his soul and that lack or that need is of son, of feeling son beloved but without the struggle to know.

The Truth Puts to Shame

The truth puts to shame those who do not seek her but she comes to them or they want to have her without truly struggling for her and that way know her, know her by not doing for her. The good thing about the truth is that she is not like those things which are found, put in store and forgotten.

For, in the very instant which the truth is, she is multiplied while being shared or divided and he that finds the truth, the truth he becomes.

Both will be Better Because Of It

He who put his good thoughts on paper or in a song, thus he is indirectly praising the creator and both of them will be better because of it.

When the Things of God are Known

At any moment now, my Master God will grant me more true joy of God granting me God more true knowledge of God so that I can know the true things of God and God declares me son beloved!

Without Royal Knowledge

Without true knowledge, of nothings serves the victory and the victory without true knowledge is another battle or struggle for true knowledge or acknowledgement.

Now then, the very same as above is with belief. Without true knowledge, of nothing really serves belief. Because in truth, according to the true knowledge which with one presents oneself to life, thus one in truth will be acknowledge into life!

Seeking a Dwelling Beloved

At Any Moment Now!

At any moment now, God Himself will give me more knowledge of God so that I can know in truth the things of God! And when I know in truth the things of God, thus God will call me son beloved so that I can truly triumph in the joy of God, who is my Master and my Father beloved!

God is my Master Beloved!

God is my Master beloved and how I would truly enjoy with all gladness and with all joy to be son beloved of my Master God beloved! And that is the very reason that I ask my God, who is my Master beloved, for more knowledge of God so that I with all gladness and with all joy can be son beloved of my God and my Master beloved!

Not until God Says Son Beloved

Not until God as Father has renamed or has recognized or acknowledged son beloved, all who live thus live in vanity! And those who died were not able to be victorious or overcame and they also lived in vanity! Because in truth, the great victory or overcoming in truth is to be called, to be called son beloved!

Thus, not until God as Father beloved calls one son beloved there will not be true victory!

The Good to Do

He who does not find the good to do, thus evilness will find him and will do him in.

God Will Do the Rest

The only one who must prove that there really is a God is oneself and God will really do the rest for one.

Chapter 7

The Seventh Victory

With the very first true gladness and with the very first true joy or royal joy thus one has truly overcome by truly seeking and by truly drawing near, but one does no realize it because the victory has come suddenly and there was no other to declare victory in spite of the true peace or the royal peace which one truly feels as victor. But what irony! One has truly overcome but one does not realize it because one truly lacks the knowledge of victory! Thus, in truth is like being born alive but there is no other to tell one that one has just being born alive or that one truly has just arrived!

Even so, one truly begins with gladness and with joy so that with gladness and joy complete what one has begun and one has begun true or royal life!

Now then, true life or true salvation of God is only received from God but true life or true salvation of God is received from God with all gladness and with all joy! And if that gladness and if that joy of God is not in one, then one will not be able to be reborn in life or in life receive acknowledgement of God so that one continues with life or one continues alive in salvation and as a true savior.

In that Good Day of Encounter

He who finds not what to do, that he truly seeks he who truly did all things! He who does not know how to do, thus that he seeks God! And if he honestly seeks God, thus God will allow to be found by him! And in that good day of encounter, he will truly know what to do and because of truly doing, thus he also will be reborn into royal life and for being reborn into royal life, royal life he also will have!

As the One Who has Drank

Many who have, they get drunk so that they can enjoy what they have. And those who do not have, they get drunk to enjoy as the one who has drank.

When the Judge will be Seen

Not until the good judge truly knows the why of the why, then the good judge will not be seen. That is to say, without true knowledge there cannot be true judgment and much less there is true liberty given. And many come out in liberty but they do not feel justified because justice has not justified them for the lack of the voice of the good judge, even though the good judge was present.

To Become Right in Evilness

He who really becomes accustomed doing certain evilness alone, thus he also will really become accustomed in group or before the people and that way justify himself or become right, right in evilness.

That is to say, there truly are many who justify themselves as righteous through the evilness of others even though those who justify themselves have not done one good.

He who is not born in joy

He who was not born in joy, thus for him becomes very difficult, nearly impossible, to do even for himself! And if he does not do the very minimum for himself, thus he will never have true knowledge to be reborn, but this time be reborn with so much joy that it will shine from his very soul!

The Word Takes One

One does not get alone to God, for one has to listen or to read the word because the word takes and brings one alive to God. The dead do not get to God, but the blind, the mute, the deaf and even the sinners, as long as they repent and they come alive through the word.

That which is Hypocrisy

He who does not know what is hypocrisy, thus he cannot keep away from her and even much less can he truly join to God. Because in truth, hypocrisy in one departs God from one!

Hypocrisy is a sack filled with vanity and he who carries it will never have the truth and even much less he will in truth see in truth which is he!

The Human Vessel

The human soul is a vessel or is female and she is filled with the truth which is also female. Now then, every vessel is to do something with her, more as to be filled with her than as to fill her. The human vessel is so refreshing as the very water because the water is a refreshing vessel which fills in truth. And the human vessel refreshes and fills God in truth.

The human soul is the only vessel which can really know God and to really know God was to really revive God.

Foundation in Doctrine

In truth, no form can be given to a foundation with doctrine because when the first wall is put up thus everything falls and even the wall is damaged. And the wall in truth is one.

The Impulse to Have

To have is in truth the impulse of having more, more in double the abundance which truly are five times the royal quantity and not to have because there is not or there is lack.

Thus those who already have, they truly want more. And those who have not, those truly want not because they have not yet tasted to have through having.

In other words, not until one has, one will not know if one wants more. And the very same thing is with life. Not until one has life, thus one will never know if one wants more and if one wants more thus all that one has to do is ask for more from the life giver, who lively he will give more life. But ask for life in life, for death only asks for more death so that one can remain dead when dead…

Nothing in the Beginning

If there were nothing in the beginning, then it cannot be started again with the same. For in truth, to give form to nothing or to lack was because there was to give with and nothing is also something, something like the beginning of putting what was lacking and what was lacking was something, but that something already was, only that it was not in nothing…

Dead in life

He who holds anger to the dead, thus he himself is dead in life and he himself smells as if already dead.

The Reality Which Is Not

Nothing truly is easy. It is not easy to establish true peace in a cave because what truly is heard are echoes of the reality which is not.

What the Father Saw

When after a long time, a son returns to his father with open arms but his father only sees the empty hands of the son, thus the father sees what the father never gave to his son and will never give.

When Love Never Reached

When a son comes to his loving father empty-handed, thus it is very obvious that the love of the father never reached the son.

The Other Who Believes Different

He who in reality does not believe or he who does not know how to believe in truth but he believes that he believes, thus he forever will say that it is the other who believes different. And he who says that the other believes different thus he who says is only a hypocrite because the hypocrisy does not know how to believe.

Now then, only a hypocrite rolls on pride as if mud and that way also disfiguring his belief without even realizing it.

The Riches of No Value

Of no value in truth are riches and honor if one hates another for simply being poor or for simply having more than one has.

Knowing Renews as Joy

True knowledge or true understanding also renews as true joy. Now, temporary joy is for evil but true joy is for the good because true joy is forever as also is the good.

Alive but Denies

It is easier for God to raise and give salvation to a dead man than to save a man alive but denies salvation of God. But God truly prefers to save the living for living and not the dead for dead. Because in truth, salvation of God is only for the living who in truth salvation of God truly desire and for salvation of God truly ask of God.

Chapter 8

Gladness and Joy

Without the true peace of God in one alive, there is no true knowledge of God. Without the true knowledge of God in one alive, there is no true gladness of God and there is neither true joy of God in one. And without the true joy of God in one alive, then truly there is not or in truth there will not be rebirth of God neither will there be rebirth of one in life, which in truth is to be reborn alive in the true salvation of God.

Now then, the true gladness of God and the true joy of God in one truly is the purpose of life or of the salvation of God in life. That is to say, the true gladness of God and the true joy of God are what truly maintain and revive life. The true gladness of God and the true joy of God is what truly transforms the circle of life into a double circle or into an eight or into a symbol of infinity which also resemble an eight, eight which also signifies or which truly reflects being beloved of God for once one truly feeling true gladness of God and the true joy of God in one for one truly seeking of God to truly believe in God or to have true knowledge of God.

Thus in truth, without that true gladness of God and without that true joy of God in one, which in truth is being beloved of God, there will not be rebirth in life, which is in truth the salvation of God, thus one will stop from being forever, even though one is beloved of God.

When One Comes to Know

When truly one comes to know or truly one comes to understand the things of God, thus God Himself in truth will let one oneself know or understand but with all true gladness and with all true joy of God!

Well then, to truly come to know or to truly come to understand was in truth to enter into the tent of the Master and because of that knowing or because of that understanding the Master will fill one with true gladness of the Master and with true joy of the Master so that both give rebirth to one in life.

Seeking a Dwelling Beloved

Possible Evidence

Possible evidence is not any evidence at all. Possible evidence is but a catch to sell as many lies as possible and lies, even a single lie, lay one in a very deep grave and that very deep grave is one for believing lies.

He Who Does for Another

If one does not do for another, then do not ask why the other does not do for one because he who does for another thus also he does for himself. But always do first for oneself so that one can do in truth for another and one waits for nothing from the other.

That it stays not in Silence

My God beloved and my Master that our wonderful encounter no longer stays in this deep silence! Because in truth, because this deep silence afflicts me and I lack your loving consul!

My God beloved and my Master, I miss you so as a son misses his loving father who has gone and who has left him in desolation!

Master my God, for your true love toward your beloved, please call me once more and this time I will respond!

The Word is His Fact

The word in truth is to explain, to understand and to see the labor done which no one as of yet has seen. He who truly does, thus his word is his fact and he now does not have to sit down to write.

So That It Can Be Responded

Creation in truth is proof of a call and according to what one has done in creation, thus one will understand and one will see and one will be called so that this time one can respond and be saved as savior beloved.

Wisdom and Her Two Sides

Wisdom of heart has two sides, one to make the foolish wiser; but if he wants not, then the more foolish! The other side is to make the wise wiser and glorify God for being wise!

God and Period

God and period is no fragment. God and period is more than complete. And for being more than complete, God renews as creator and as much more than creator.

Understanding and Victory

Understanding is victory because understanding is really standing in the tent of the loving Master and waiting for a sit in.

Now then, victory is being free to work out or to sit in but the moment one walks out, there is no sit in. And to sit in is to become one with the loving Master…

Without Pleasure

Without pleasure, man would not be a living being and life, human or not, would have no single purpose; even God would be without purpose because the greatest pleasure in all creation is really God.

When a House Divides

When one argues with one's partner, thus the house becomes like two; but the second part of the house cannot be entered or found until one reconciles with one's partner. Now, both parts are united, thus making them both as one and as new.

That is to really say, when a house divides, the spirits or the gladness finds no dwelling. But when the house reunites or when the house becomes complete, the spirit becomes also refreshed or becomes as new that way forgetting the division through the addition.

With True Knowledge

Those that in truth are united are united in true knowledge or in true understanding. And with God is also the same. That is to say, those that in truth unite with God are united with true knowledge of God.

To Carry Liberty

He that is raised in obligation as if in slavery, thus to him becomes impossible to carry liberty. That is to say, he that is really accustomed to not doing, but he still receives, thus he in the very day which he no longer receives, he will die and as dead will be without knowing or be without being known. Because in truth, one enters into life as also into salvation by doing for one and that one is one.

Freedom is a Package

To one, freedom is very sweet. But to another, the idea of being free simply brings another fear, another package and another useless burden.

The Test Clay Vases

All living men as well as all living women are test clay vases or test tubes. And they both will be tested according to what they already know and not to what not.

And all dead men as well as all dead women have both failed the clay test.

The Wits which is Killed With

When the enemy cannot kill one, thus the enemy uses one's wits. And it is truly with one's wits that the enemy really kills with. Thus, the enemy destroys one with what one already knows.

He that is Not Judged

He that knows not or that has not true knowledge thus neither is he judged. But he that says not to know thus he has knowledge that he knows not and he will be judged besides himself. And also, he that says he knows not, he already has being judged for he has knowledge that he knows not. That is, he knows that he does not know.

A Vase of Honor

Man is the only clay vase that really speaks, but he uses his speech to complain instead of praising the clay maker. And according to the praise, the clay maker could praise back and rename the clay vase a preferred vase, a vase of honor. For in truth, the son beloved of God will come out because of praise…

Wisdom for Wisdom

A man can hear the wisdom of another but only God can teach wisdom for wisdom from God through understanding. In other words, to understand thus one must first do but the wisdom of God teaches without doing.

Now then, the wisdom of God is the only wisdom that can be really understood without doing. The thing is that only those who seek God, God allow that wisdom of God.

Chapter 9

The Salvation of God

True salvation or the salvation of God is for those that are alive and alive are reborn in life. True salvation or the salvation of God is in truth to maintain life in the double and true abundance of God and with the double and true abundance of God thus with life in life in truth be able to continue. But that continuation of life is in truth with perfect or true peace of God and with perfect or true knowledge of God and with perfect or true gladness of God and with perfect or true joy of God and also the salvation of God is with perfect or true power of God and with perfect or true authority of God over life, which now is the real salvation or the true salvation or the salvation of God.

Now then, true salvation or the salvation of God thus has nothing to do in truth with death or with after death or with dying that first death. All of those that were born dead thus in truth lost the very great opportunity to life and because of not having life thus will not be able to be reborn alive or will not be able to receive the salvation of God or true salvation.

And also, all of those that died or that die after being born, thus all of those also lost the very great opportunity of being reborn or alive in life or of receiving the true salvation of God or true salvation. Thus in truth, the salvation of God or true salvation is for the living and that want to continue living and they ask it from God to continue alive. That is, to continue alive is truly the salvation of God. And the true salvation of God is true abundance of God in one alive.

Thus in truth, to receive the salvation of God or true salvation or real salvation thus one has to come to truly believe in God but for oneself. And to come to truly believe in God for oneself thus one must seek God so that with that search, one comes to truly believe in God or one comes to have true faith of God. One will know in truth when one feels a true gladness and a true joy which never were in one before. That gladness and that joy, which are both true, is the loving grace or is the presence of God in one. That loving grace in one puts one in the state of beloved, of beloved of God!

In that state of beloved of God, one can hear a voice promising something useful like promising a better life or one can feel often a lot of true gladness and a lot of true joy or even both. But one cannot continue much longer for a long time in that new state of beloved of God because eventually will come the departure of the loving grace or of the gleeful presence. That departure of God from one or of God from beloved of God takes one in truth into the desolation of God, which is in truth to feel now contrary to the loving grace. That is, in this new state of desolation, one feels afflicted and one also lacks the loving consul or the real knowledge or the true knowledge of God.

In this state of desolation of God, thus one as beloved of God must once again seek for God, but one as beloved of God must in truth seek of God as Father and one as son! Because in truth, without the true knowledge or rename from God to one as son beloved of God, thus in truth there is no salvation of God!

With What One Brings

No one wins a prize for not being born and much less for dying. It is truly given to one with what one truly brings into life. And in life is the very same. One truly receives more life according to what one has done with life so that with life one can receive more life.

And he that arrives dead, thus dead he stays. And he that dies, thus also he stays dead!

That which is of God

That which is truly of God thus one must truly do to truly see it and truly forget it not and it truly becomes also forever new because truly it will be the very truth of God.

Soon It Will Be Granted to Me!

My God and my Master beloved, I know that you truly know my struggle to know your things of God and soon now you yourself will allow me more real knowledge so that I can truly know and that way you God beloved declare me son beloved so that way also I can overcome and triumph in your true joy as it is your good pleasure as loving Father.

Yes, my God and my Master beloved, I truly know that you truly know my great struggle to truly know your things of God and soon now you will grant me true knowledge of son beloved of the Master!

Unity and Test

The union is a test and the union in test truly brings triumph, true gladness and true joy in double abundance of God. And the greater part of the union is truly one and not the other even though the other is the other half of the union. And the greater part of one is God because God is true pleasure and true joy and that is truly what God has for one for one.

In One as One

The majority of beliefs have certain truths but the conflicts or the chaos truly is when they forget that the truth becomes complete in one as one and one alive.

The Knowledge of One

Chaos is truly the lack of true knowledge, thus true knowledge is truly what gives form and the more true knowledge of one, thus more form one has. Thus, if one does not have true knowledge of one, then one is not one.

Grant Me More Royal Knowledge!

Master God beloved, for your great love toward your beloved, please grant me more true knowledge so that I can truly do and can truly know and can truly respond this time through your true form!

Because in truth, one seeks the form to respond even though the voice is very clear!

I Will Lack Nothing!

Oh, let that which is of God reign in my life! Oh, let that which is of God reign in my life because truly God is my Master beloved and noting truly I will lack, not ever!

Oh, let that which is of God reign in my life! Oh, let that which is of God reign in my life because truly God is my joy and my pleasure! Because God is my true knowledge and my true understanding! Because God is my victory declared and my royal triumph!

Oh, let that which is of God reign in my life because God is my double and royal abundance and truly nothing I will ever lack! Because God is truly my royal victory and in God with all joy I will truly triumph!

God Knows One

God has allowed one to know allowing God to be known. God knows one allowing God to be known. And according to the knowledge given to God, thus God truly knows one.

God knows one allowing one to know God for God is true knowledge as also God is true understanding. And since God is true knowledge as also God is true understanding, thus also God will allow to be truly known and truly in more wisdom of heart.

Thus in truth, God knows one through the very same knowledge that one has of God and the more true the knowledge that one has of God, thus the more one will be to God.

Now and as New

When truly the joy of God arrives to one, to one that was never happy and that always suffered, thus now one is as if one never was unhappy and one is also as if one had never truly suffered because one truly was reborn and now as also forever one is as new and also as if two…

And I Will be the Truth

In that wonderful day, when I truly smile with the smile of son beloved and I dare to be completely joyful with the true joy of my father that is truly in the heavens, I, through the will of God, will know and I will see the truth and the truth I will be…

Because in truth to smile as son beloved through the joy of the father was the good work of the good servant!

It is Not When One Says

It is truly when God says and not when one says, even though one may be right. And that is true faith. But because that is true faith, one will not stop requesting God that with all gladness and with all joy gives and that truly gives!

But in truth, what God gives or what God truly grants are the power and the authority of one oneself to do for what one truly desires. That is truly, God gives or God grants to one the good ability to do so that with the work of one, thus one can truly see and truly have through the desire or through the lack of one.

Because in truth, everything that one had or everything that one received without doing for, thus everything truly will be forgotten and because of being forgotten, things become lost. But what is done for by one, forever will be one's…

Authority in Truth

Of nothing serves faith or belief if truly does not take or does not come the power and the authority of being reborn in life and in truth.

The Law without Authority

Of nothing serves to study or to understand the law if truly there is no authority to truly complete the law in true justice. And true justice is that justice which renews all, as much as the accused, as much as the accuser and as much as those that interpret the law.

God Will Grant Me

God is truly my peace and my true knowledge and for my requesting, God will grant me true peace and true knowledge of God because without the knowledge from God toward me, thus in truth there will not be salvation of God for me!

One Knows Oneself More

One truly knows oneself more truly knowing God and truly knowing God thus one is as God and even more through God because God truly will make one the preferred vase of God.

To Know the Lack

To come to truly know the lack is in truth the beginning of knowing the double abundance which in truth is five times the amount.

The True Abundance

Now soon now, God will grant me true knowledge of so that I can truly see the double true abundance and the double true abundance I can with all gladness and with all joy enjoy giving all grace to God!

The Knowledge of God

The knowledge of God is truly good because the knowledge of God brings true faith and because of true faith, the believer is renewed more than once until he is touched by the salvation of God and through her, the good believer will be renewed forever as savior beloved of God.

The Unknown Struggle

The more difficult is to know the struggle, thus longer and thus harder or more difficult will that unknown struggle be. Thus to be able to truly overcome, one needs true knowledge and true knowledge is asked for from he that grants true knowledge. And the only one that truly can grant true knowledge to do and to overcome is only God but God does not grant if of God is not asked or requested.

Chapter 10

Dwelling

According to the true knowledge given or granted through the true knowledge which one oneself presented for being born alive, thus one oneself will do for oneself and for what one has done or will do in life, thus one will present oneself again alive in life with that very same and true knowledge, true knowledge because truly one has done alive in life with that knowledge.

And for what one has truly done or according to how the very facts themselves speak for one, thus one will have the very great opportunity of truly being dwelling of God. And when one becomes the dwelling of God through the very request of one, thus one has being reborn again with the spirit or with the gladness of God in one.

Now then, that new rebirth is truly a second salvation of God or resurrection of God because now one as dwelling of God has being reborn or one has resuscitated in the spirit or with the gladness of God when one was reborn the first time, thus one was reborn in the spirit or with the gladness of son beloved of God.

The Royal Knowledge of Son

Where is my loving God and my Master beloved the knowledge of son which a request so that I can truly do and because of doing thus truly know as son your things of God? And when I, as son, truly know your thing of God, you declare me son beloved so that I can overcome this struggle to know as son beloved and be able to triumph in your joy as son beloved of the Master as is your good pleasure of God.

Where is my loving God and my Master beloved the knowledge of son which I request from you? Because in truth, if you my Master God beloved do not grant me knowledge of son, thus I will surely die for lack of knowledge and forever we will be apart from one another!

You Are My Salvation

How much lovelier and how much joy would be my life, my loving God and my Master beloved, if only I could hear your voice telling me, I, God your God, am your salvation! Oh, and that loving God will complete my joy and would also make me feel again as in the very heavens! And this time united to you my loving God and my Master beloved for all the times!

To Believe in Truth

To truly believe is truly to take out from what is to come and be able to put where there was not before. For in truth, to believe was truly to create…

When It Becomes Impossible Already Having

When some need, they seek he that truly has even though it may be the very minimum and no one seeks he who does not have. And they even do the impossible to seek that which is of another. But when they come to have for themselves, they also do the impossible to not share, not even the very minimum of the true joy which truly completes no matter how small the possession that one may have.

The Green Fruit

He that does not know the green fruit, thus he will not be able to acknowledge or to recognize the fruit as ripe. And he that does not know the fruit neither green nor ripe, he will neither know the seed.

To Die Is Not To Do

One must first do to truly know things which are already known but which are not seen and to wait and to die is not to do no matter how good the doctrine sounds. Because in truth, too much sound from the river is too much sound of the water and too much sound from the river does not sound too good.

Of What Was Is What Is

Of what truly was thus it is and what will truly come will truly come because it truly is. That is, it is truly formed or it is given true knowledge from what truly is or from what truly has arrived. Because in truth, what really arrives brings true knowledge but true knowledge of what already really was.

When Are You Going To Fatten Me?

My Master and my God beloved, when are you going to fatten me with the oil from your true joy which renews man and also renews God? When, my Master beloved?

To Do, To Learn, To Understand

It is not the question whether someone teaches so that the other can learn or understand but rather it is the question that one as the other must first do to learn to understand.

Now then, only through one truly doing can one truly know.

Now then, to come to truly know is to be reborn alive into abundance of life. Thus, to come to truly know was to enter back into life but as if new and as if new forever and as if one never ever left the loving and abundant grace of the Father…

When Death Comes To An End

When there is no more death, also there will not be any more error and no killing but so that death truly ends, in life one has to truly seek and to truly know the life giver that gives true life through really knowing.

To Create and To Form

To create and to form are not the same for to form was from what already was and to create was to take out from what never was even though there was one. It only was created but once and all the rest was formed.

So God formed man with what already was and did not do a second creation for man. For, to form was truly to name alive so that with the name, form can be taken and the form is really proof of creation, of creation through name.

Now then, it was created only once, the rest was given form through simple living name.

Proving God to Others

Proving God to others is very rough and nearly impossible but not to oneself. And that is the very reason that one must be true to oneself, for the truth is one…

Saturday and the True Rest

Saturday, which is a day of victory, is a true rest of giving true form or of giving name in the joy of God so that both parts become new and the next day also becomes for all times new.

Death and the Not Complete

When one dies thus it was because one was not complete. That is, when one dies it was because one was not completed by he that completes one. And when one dies, one dies for lack of being completed in life. And only God will complete in life so that one dies not…

Vase Filled In Vain

A vase filled not recognized filled thus is known as an empty vase and it is a vase filled in vain and what is in it will spoil and rotten and will also turn to dust, the end of form. And such is the cup of victory when not refilled or not refreshed by its maker because man is the cup of victory when man is reborn or born again but in life…

To Truly Believe Is To Give Form

To create or to do, as also is to believe, is to truly take out from what will come and put where there was not, that way to give form. Because in truth, form cannot be given to what is not known and not seen even though it is.

To Be Reborn To Never Die

Many are born in truly gladness and in true joy but know it not for they were not told. But to know true gladness and true joy is to be reborn to never die. Now then, true gladness and true joy are of God and God never dies and that is the very reason one must seek God because God will put true gladness and true joy in one. In fact, one will be God's true gladness and true joy!

The Best Sound

Sometimes, the best sound is the one not heard because of hearing thus one seeks the sound and because of seeking thus one stops from hearing and because of not hearing thus one responded not to what could had being from very deep inside of one.

Cured and saved

Whether one is cured and saved is not the same. Faith of God is the cure as also is the salvation of God. But faith alone saves not even though it is faith of God. Only God saves but when one is cured with the faith of God.

Chapter 11

Adding and Becoming

One by one is what one gets through one. One comes to life through one and through one thus one truly adds to life as one and also one adds to life to keep alive. And if one truly adds to life, one also truly adds to God and when one truly adds to God, God truly becomes more as one also becomes truly more and more is God as Father and more is one as son, son beloved of God.

Now then, to be able to be more than one is to truly add to the creation of God. And to be able to truly add to the creation of God is to become the right hand of God.

Thus, for every one true part that one puts or that one truly shows thus an exact amount will be truly given or granted so that one can truly have double the abundance of God and through the double abundance of God, one do again or one do as new.

Joy Adds Joy

Water tastes much better when there truly is thirst. And true gladness and true joy is added when true gladness and true joy was started with because true gladness and true joy truly renew or give rebirth in double abundance.

The Dead Philosophy of Man

The philosophy of man was always dead because dead was born the philosophy of man but soon the Great Philosopher that invented true knowledge will bury the dead philosophy of man and will give rebirth to the philosophy of God so that man can live life and no longer fantasies about death.

Believe and Opportunity

To believe is not to know or is not to understand. To believe truly is a great opportunity of requesting to know and also of be known or acknowledged. Because in truth, without the acknowledgement from above from the heavens there is not rebirth of man and of God!

Light and Knowledge

Light is true knowledge and as true knowledge, light does not have to say it is light or that light is. Because in truth, God gave the light true knowledge of light so that through her the things of God would be complete and the glory of God would be seen in them as the glory of God is seen as the light…

The Positive and the Irrational

If ever there were a rat to think and that thinking were positive that rat would be irrational.

Positive Thinking and the Hypocrite

Positive thinking only works for those who already have plenty even if it is what belongs to one! And one can tell when someone is a hypocrite when he says to be positive. Also, watch out for free stuff for it may be stealing your precious time! The hypocrite gets to an intersection but he turns back. Keep far away from hypocrites and their useless positive thinking!

The Light and Rebirth

The light is so that one does, one knows and one is reborn. And when one is reborn, one will be new but one as if two because now God dwells in one.

Struggle without Knowing

He that struggles without knowing or without understanding thus it is as if he did not struggle or the struggle is in vain. Because in truth, through true knowledge is given and through true knowledge is overcome and is triumphed.

Life Equals Plus

Life equals understanding or life is truly about knowing plus the abundance of joy of God. Anything else is but vanity! Because in truth, the joy of God in one not only gives rebirth to one but also the joy of God in one gives God rebirth and therefore renewing the earth as the very heavens…

The Good and the Bad

The good is accused of doing many bad things but the bad of only being bad.

God Is a Struggle

God is a struggle to know or to acknowledge before time expires. And if one acknowledges God, God will acknowledge one as beloved of God and extend one's life as beloved and as beloved of God, one could also be acknowledged savior beloved of God if one acknowledges God savior beloved of God. Because in truth, from one as beloved of God one will become savior beloved of God!

Vessel of Another

A brother never should be a mule or a vessel of another but rather inspiration even though a minor brother! Thus in truth, one has to be a vessel first if a vessel is needed…

To Struggle with What Cannot Be Seen

It is much easier to struggle or to fight with what can be seen and is. But to truly struggle or to truly fight with what cannot be seen thus one needs true knowledge so that with true knowledge present oneself and be seen and see oneself for more because for more one presented to the world and the world became more because of one.

When Something Is Complete

One can truly tell when something is complete when it can be added more through good words. And only man alive as well as God can do such a good deed, truly add to things already complete…

A Gift without Obligation

Wisdom of heart returns but only returns to he that was, is and will be wise. And being wise is a lovely gift from God without obligation toward God. Also, wisdom of heart is a very loving consul from God and also without obligation toward God. But if there is no grace in the mouth of the wise after the wisdom of heart, thus the wise is wise in vanity.

The Tests of God

The tests of God are not to make one, that is beloved of God, fail or to afflict more than usual but the tests of God are to make one, that is beloved of God, thus be justified or so that one as beloved of God becomes righteous.

Now then, he that died, thus truly he died because he lived in vain because he did not truly seek God, he was not placed as beloved of God in passing the tests of God.

Once again I say to you, the tests of God truly are not test so that man, who is beloved of God, fails! However, even though a fighter, man fails! And that very failure of man thus takes man to death which is eternal punishment and where God does not remember the dead for the dead being dead. Because in truth, for the dead there are no longer tests and they have already proven that they failed with death and in death no dead is justified because justification of God or being pronounced righteousness is in life herself and by God himself.

Belief and the Blind

Everything that one believes is not good. In truth, the very belief leaves one blind and besides if the belief of one depends on one thus it will truly have great failure! Because in truth, true belief is of God and because of God is that one truly believes!

When One Arrives is Because One Already Was
Water runs and runs and fills and fills but the water knows it not. However, without knowing, water arrives for water because water always was. Thus, noting arrives that never was.

Wisdom Will Return
Wisdom of heart is of God as the truth is of God. And as wisdom of heart comes thus wisdom of heart goes but wisdom of heart will return if waited for as waited for God.

When Peace Becomes a Bore
When the peace of man becomes a bore, it brings the war of man! But the peace of God, which is true peace, thus brings true knowledge of God and true knowledge of God also brings true gladness and true joy of God and true gladness and true joy of God gives rebirth to one so that one continues as new in all truth as the very truth!

Chapter 12

On The Right Side

According to the true knowledge of life that one presented at birth, thus one truly does and one is truly known through that very same knowledge of life and one will also respond for oneself when one is called to be acknowledged into life and to the right side of God.

One will not respond for what some other did or for what some other says that he did for one because what some other did, that other did for himself through the true knowledge of life that the other presented at birth and being born for the other. And if the other overcame or was reborn in life, thus the other only did if for the other and no one else.

Now then, one will be reborn in life also through the very same true knowledge of life which one presents in life. And to be reborn or to overcome truly was to receive knowledge through knowledge and that rebirth or that overcoming cannot be given to another because it is only for one for what one has truly done or for one's very true effort to know or of one given knowledge or acknowledgement.

Thus in truth, according to the true knowledge or true acknowledgement of one thus also one will be called to life or called into life and put at the right side of God as the very right arm of God. This truly does not indicate that one will go to some other side, such as the heavens or nothing like that, but that one will be as if new and because of feeling as if new thus one will feel as if one has just arrived as if from another side and one will be here as if in the very heavens!

True Wisdom

True wisdom of God or wisdom of heart, as everything else that is true only comes from God the loving creator. God the creator gives or grants for free true wisdom of God or wisdom of heart to all of those who seek God and ask of God or who request so that their souls, which is life, can be filled with righteousness and their spirits, which is the conscious mind, can truly be renewed with the true joy of God, the loving creator.

Complete Belief

To believe is not truly a fact much less truly understanding or truly knowing. To truly understand, one must first do or know. What is already done takes one to true knowledge and true knowledge after doing or knowing takes one to understanding which is into the tent of the good Master Creator.

Only in understanding can be believed for understanding is doing or knowing. Therefore, if belief becomes not, then it is not a complete belief. And complete belief takes one again to the wonderful tent or to the living grace of the good Master Creator.

God Waits

God truly waits for those who truly wait for God and their waiting, even though long, will not be in vain for they will be truly called and when they respond, they need not wait anymore and they will be as new for responding and as if they never ever waited.

To Believe Is Not To Know

One cannot please God without true understanding or without true knowledge because to believe is not to understand or to know. Because in truth, one truly believes with the knowledge that one presented oneself and if there is answer after one presenting oneself, then through that very same answer is that truly one has come to truly believe, truly understand or truly know.

Because in truth, true knowledge, which allows one to truly believe or have true faith, truly gives and truly receives form.

True Faith Speaks For the Believer

True belief or true faith of God is that which is already complete and one is in as if in a new state. And if one is in, then it is obvious and one does not have to mention that one believes. If the belief is not a fact or is not complete, then the belief or the faith is a borrowed belief or is a borrowed faith and it will never be complete, it will never be a fact or it will never be obvious.

Because in truth, true belief or faith of God speaks for one as it speaks for God because it came from God as the first gift from God.

To Be Joyful Is the Reward

To do good without obligation is to be glad and joyful with true gladness and with true joy and to be truly glad and truly joyful with true gladness true joy is the grandiose reward because through true gladness and true joy one is reborn in life.

Now, true gladness and true joy both come from God and both are granted by God as an acknowledgement from God because of one drawing near to God.

The One That Speaks Too Much

The one that truly knows a lot is the one that truly keeps silent and the one that knows very little or does not know, thus speaks too much!

The Cry Baby and the Cub

He that is very silly is very much a cry baby; and he that is very much a cry baby is a cub.

What God Has For His Beloved

God does not ask from his beloved of God because what God has for his beloved of God is so great that it serves them both.

It Is Impossible To Do Nothing

It is impossible for a living person to do nothing; for if he breathes, he is doing something; if he sees, is he doing something; and if he thinks, is he doing something and perhaps is he completing something.

What Is Done Brings Knowledge

One day, true belief or faith of God will be done or will be fact because even though true belief or faith of God is to know but it cannot be understood without doing. For, what is truly done brings true knowledge and through the truth, the things of God will be known and will be seen. And the truth will be one when God says so that through one, one can know and one can see the things of God.

Positive and Negative

What is positive for one can be very negative for another. And the negative of another can be because that other is low or below. And the positive of one is because he is high or above and can see beyond.

He that is in the highest only sees what is in the highest but there are not too many things high that can be seen. And what is below, which can be very negative to another, cannot only see what is below but can also see what is between the low and the high and can even see the very high. Thus, he that only thinks through one mode, thus his one-sided tower truly will fall!

Knowledge Brings a Better View

He that thinks of only one manner, thus to him his tower of Babylon will fall! For, it is required to truly improve the point of view so that it can be known and knowledge brings a much better view or a much better form.

Gladness Does Not Enter Where It Is Not Invited

The spirit or the living gladness does not enter where it is not known, where the spirit itself knows not or where the spirit is not waited for. That is, the spirit which is sigh or breath does not enter by itself. That spirit or the living gladness needs to be invited and where there is for it a space so that it can truly enter. And the same is truly with the good spirit or the good gladness of God. The good spirit or the good gladness of God does not enter where it is not known and neither enter where it truly is not waited for with a special place or dwelling.

That Which Is True Faith

Faith is to believe in something great that already is but it cannot be seen. But to be able to see it, thus one truly has to do. Because in truth, by doing thus the things are known and by knowing the things thus the things also are formed and the things are seen.

Thus, a son that is not born cannot see the greatness of the father that also is not because through the very birth of the son, the father was reborn! And because the father was reborn through the very birth of his son, the son is beloved of the father and through the true love of the father; the son will also be reborn when the father renames his son, son beloved. And that rebirth of the son beloved of the father will also make the father greater because the father was reborn once again into a greater father or father beloved of the son beloved of the father beloved.

To Be Able To See the Abundance

My God and my Master beloved, please grant me that knowledge of son beloved that I request so that I can see the abundance that you are that you have promised me and also I can be joyful with all joy in her!

That From Above Returns Above

That which is from above not too often is seeing, not too often is understood and not too often comes to one; but when it comes, thus enjoy it with complete joy to the possible maximum because that which is from above returns to that above.

Not Until It Is Understood

Not until it is truly understood as to the why, thus one truly cannot enjoy completely the abundance and much less share it and multiply it. But to truly understand which was truly to enter once again into the wonderful tent of the loving Master, thus one has to truly know! And one truly knows through rebirth as once one was truly born. And one was truly born through truly doing.

Through The Few Belonging To Another

He that worries not for the very little which belongs to another, thus neither will he worry for much and he will never have not even the very minimum for himself. Because in truth, life does not belong to one until from above is truly declared!

Conclusion

To come in truth to understand or to know in truth was to come in truth to enter again with true peace and with true knowledge and with true gladness and with true joy in one as one and enter in one complete in truth or enter into one as the complete truth. That is to say, to come to understand was to be reborn as the very truth and in complete harmony.

Because the truth is that one once came out from the loving grace with true peace and with true knowledge and with true gladness and with true joy and even with true and double abundance but one knew it not until one was born and born alive. And for being born alive, one truly presented oneself with true knowledge which oneself brought of life to those that waited in the world for one alive, thus those that waited in the world for one and because of the knowledge of one alive, they with true gladness and with true joy and with true abundance in truth conformed!

That is to truthfully say, that one was known with what one truly brought into the world and if one brought true knowledge of life thus true knowledge of life also was given to one by the world. Well now, with that true knowledge, one has to truly do to be able to truly know or to truly remember the loving grace so that through the loving grace one can bring into the world with true peace and with true knowledge and with true gladness and with true joy be reborn or be truly recognized as once one was known for being born alive and bringing also true knowledge of live into the world.

Once again, when one is born alive, one brings true knowledge of life thus one is also truly known and according to what one truly does in life with the true knowledge given for the very same knowledge of one thus one will do or also one will present oneself. And according to how one will present oneself as once one did by being born alive, thus one will receive more true knowledge so that one with that true knowledge can be known again or one can truly be reborn alive in life or into life.

Now then, to be reborn alive is to truly receive the true knowledge of life which is truly to receive the true knowledge of salvation or receive the true knowledge of son beloved of God!

One more time, all of us believers are truly beloveds of God and because of being beloveds of God thus we truly are in desolation of God which is truly to be away from the loving grace or from the presence for lack of true knowledge of son beloved of God. To be able to come out or exit from the desolation of God, thus one truly must request God to grant us the true knowledge of son beloved of God because the knowledge of son beloved of God will take us from the very desolation of God and will put us in the true salvation of God!

Thus very good luck with true salvation of God and with the royal dwelling or with the true dwelling of God! May God truly bless you all with the true knowledge of son beloved of God if it is that the true knowledge of son beloved of God you truly desire and you truly request from God so that God truly grants it to you!

Closing Notes

I am one of those, and perhaps the only one in these very difficult times, who with complete sincerity seeks the truth of the universe, the truth of the creation of God and the truth of what is really the salvation of man and man, as far as I know, will not be saved from eternal death by the technology of man as neither the very sword will save man. Technology as the sword will only save man temporarily. And technology can also be a double edge sword or contra productive because man does not really use it to expand or to really increase his time or to expand or to really increase his real knowledge.

My search for the truth of the universe, for the truth of the creation of God and for the truth of what is really the salvation of man has been very good to me, so good in fact that it has taken me to not only achieve or to have real faith of God but also my search has allowed me to really understand what is in truth the salvation of man by God, the good and loving creator. And the very simple truth is that without real knowledge of God, thus there will not be the salvation of God and without the salvation of God, thus there will neither be the salvation of man nor will there be the salvation of the universe, because as man will return eternally dead to the very dust, thus also the universe will return to nothing…

Thus, in my very simple writings, there are certain truths or real knowledge of life! Glad and joyful, he who in truth lends real or royal attention!

To be continued…

Seeking a Dwelling Beloved